BRIGHT STARS
DARK SKIES
Exploring space with Elijah

Elijah Leon Paul

Disclaimer

This book is a collection of facts and information about space that I, Elijah Leon Paul, have learned from reading books, watching videos, and exploring online sources. None of the information or discoveries in this book are my own. I have done my best to remember and share the things I find exciting about space, but due to my age, I may not recall every source. The images in this book are for illustration purposes only and may not represent the actual appearance or scale of space objects. They are intended to help young readers visualize these fascinating concepts but should not be considered scientific representations. If you find your work here, please do not be offended. I acknowledge and appreciate your contributions to space science and thank you for inspiring young readers like me. I hope this book sparks curiosity in other kids and encourages them to learn more about our amazing universe.

Author(Compiled by): Elijah Leon Paul

Book mentor and design: Vajeda Kardar

Self published by: Elijah Leon Paul

www.author.elijahleon@gmail.com

Dedicated to

My Father

Late Mr. Paul Gracewin

Never give up on what you really want to do. The
person with big dreams is more powerful than the
person with all the facts.

-Albert Einstein

From Elijah

Hi, I'm Elijah, and I'm 8 years old. I've always been fascinated by the mysteries of space. Some kids dream of being superheroes, but my biggest dream is to become a space scientist and an astronaut, exploring places beyond Earth and seeing the stars and planets up close. I spend hours with my little telescope, just staring at the night sky, connecting the dots between the stars and trying to understand everything I've learned from books, videos, and the internet. I feel like there's a whole universe of secrets up there, waiting to be discovered.

I'm always on the lookout for anything about space! Whether it's reading books by scientists like Stephen Hawking and Albert Einstein, watching videos about galaxies, or browsing the latest space news, I just can't get enough of it. I don't remember exactly where I found each fact in this book because I didn't originally collect them to write a book. I learned these things because I wanted to know, and I found them so exciting that I wanted to share them with other kids.

I compiled this book with everything I've read or watched, to make it easy and fun for kids my age to understand the amazing things in our universe, like how Earth was formed, how stars are born and die, and even what a black hole might be like. None of these are my discoveries—they're things I've learned from great minds and sources that I admire. I tried my best to list where I found the information, but since I'm just a kid, I couldn't remember every detail. My only goal here is to help other kids learn about the wonders of the universe that our Almighty has created. I hope reading this makes you as curious and excited about space as I am!

Happy reading

Elijah Leon Paul

INDEX

1. God Gives Life

However, before that, He created Earth, a place of dwelling for humans, animals and countless organisms. He decorated the skies with stars and other celestial bodies that we call space. So, come along with me on a journey to explore the vast and deep wonders of space.

When God drew the universe he made it beautiful just right and made it realistic! He made the things move.

That's how good God is! We should love Him and obey His orders to make Him happy about His beautiful creation- US!

2. The Universe

The universe is like the biggest playground ever, where everything exists.

It's a huge space filled with stars, planets, and galaxies, and it's so big that we can't even imagine how big it is. It's where we live, along with all the other planets and stars.

Some parts of the universe are still a mystery, but scientists keep exploring it to learn more about where we come from and how everything works together.

Actual Universe
The actual universe is everything that exists, even the parts we can't see or explore yet. It's like knowing the playground is much bigger than what you can see, but you haven't gotten to the farthest edges yet.

The actual universe includes all the stars, planets, and galaxies, both the ones we know about and the ones we don't. It's like a giant mystery, where we keep discovering new things, but there's always more out there that we haven't found yet.

Observable Universe
The observable universe is the part of the universe that we can actually see or detect. It's like the area of the playground that we can explore or look at with our eyes or telescopes.

Even though the universe is much bigger, the observable universe is all we can see because light from farther away hasn't had enough time to reach us yet. So, it's like having a huge playground, but you can only explore the part that's close enough for you to see right now.

Our universe is mysterious. It is full of wonders, full of different types of planets and galaxies.

Galaxies come in a variety of shapes mostly spirals or elliptical or irregular or less orderly.

Galaxy consist of stars, planets and vast clouds of dust and matter. They are held together by gravity. The largest galaxies contains trillions of stars while the smallest can contain a few thousand stars.

In 1927, an astronomer named Georges Lemaitre said that the universe started from a single point, it stretched and expanded. This is BIG BANG THEORY

In the beginning, the universe was hot and tiny. These tiny particles mixed with light and energy and gradually cooled down and expanded. Slowly, atoms began to combine and form stars and galaxies.

Just two years later, Edwin Hubble, an American astronomer discovered that the galaxies were moving apart from each other. This meant that the universe is expanding just as Lemaitre thought.

10

According to NASA, our galaxy is called the Milky Way. It is our home galaxy. It is spiral in shape with a disc of stars spanning more than 100,000 light years.
Our solar system is a part of Milky Way galaxy.

Galaxies come in a variety of shapes mostly spirals or elliptical or irregular or less orderly.

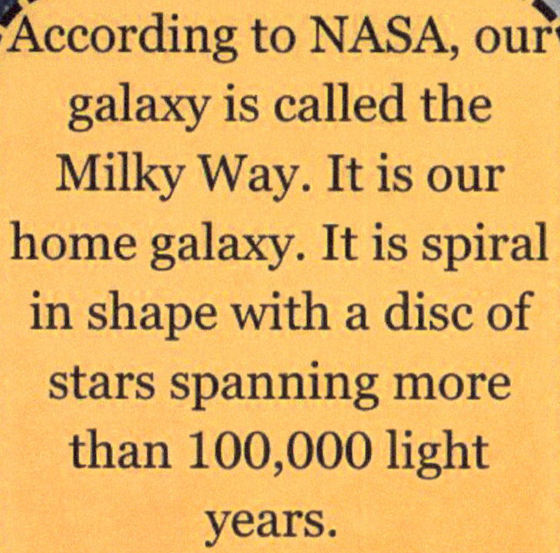

Earth

Laniakea Supercluster is a collection of over 100,000 galaxies.

The Milky way has nearly or more than 50 galaxies in its neighbourhood. This is called the Local Group. All these galaxies including our Milky Way is the part of Laniakea Supercluster

11

3. Our Solar System

Mercury is grey. It is the first and the smallest planet of our solar system.

According to NASA, Mercury is shrinking as its core is cooling and contracting. Its diameter has already shrunk by 14 kilometers since it formed about 4.5 billion years ago.

One year is just 88 days on Mercury.

Venus is second in line and sixth largest planet. It is pale yellow due to thick sulphuric acid clouds.

Earth is the third planet of our solar system. It is the fifth largest planet. Also called blue planet as it has water on its surface and atmosphere around, it appears to be blue from space.

An year on Venus is 255 Earth days

An year on Earth is 365.25 days

Mars is red due to iron oxide on its surface. It is the second smallest planet. One Martian year is about 687 Earth days

The temperature on Mars is -81 degrees Fahrenheit. Pretty COLD!

Jupiter has massive storms on its surface. The Great Red Spot is a centuries-old storm.

One year on Jupiter is 12 Earth years.

Jupiter is the biggest planet of our solar system. It has the swirls of orange, brown, yellow and white due to gases and clouds over it.

Uranus is light blue due to the methane present in its atmosphere. It is the third largest planet.

Saturn is yellowish brown with hints of gold. It is the second largest planet.

A year on Saturn is 29 Earth years.

Uranus spins sideways, on almost horizontal axis.

A year on Uranus is 84 Earth years

Saturn has rings around it. These rings are made up of billions of chunks of ice and rock.

Neptune is deep blue. It is the fourth largest planet. It is farthest from the sun.

One day on Saturn is 10.7 hours.

A year on Neptune is 165 Earth years

4. Sun- The source of light and heat

The Sun is the largest object in our solar system. It sits in the center and has a strong gravitational force that holds all the planets, asteroids and comets in orbit.

The core of the sun reaches extreme temperatures of about 27 million degrees Fahrenheit

It is made up of hydrogen and helium.

It is so huge that 1.3 million Earths could fit inside it.

It shines because nuclear reactions at its core convert hydrogen into helium releasing huge amounts of heat and light.

It takes about 8 minutes 20 seconds for sunlight to travel 93 million miles(150 million kilometers) to reach Earth.

5. History of Earth

4.5 billion years ago Earth didn't have life.

It had no water just lava and volcanoes everywhere, and more than 1000 degrees Celsius temperature.

Most scientists assumed that it took more than 500 million years for the earth to cool down

Later, earth transformed into a habitable planet

The first living things were microscopic organism, this is what we have learnt in our schools and heard from elders. Plants evolved later.

According to NASA, the distance by which the Earth orbits the sun is just perfect for water to remain in a liquid state. This distance from the sun is called the habitable zone or the goldilocks zone.
Too hot
Habitable zone
Our planet Earth lies in the habitable zone of the universe
Too cold

6
THINK ZONE
What do you think is the similarity between an ocean and space?

Well, I think...

Fish in the sea are similar to stars and planets in the space. They both shimmer and move gracefully in their respective environments.

As you go deeper inside the ocean, it is dark because the sunlight cannot reach there. Similarly, beyond earth's atmosphere, the space too is dark with only the light from stars

Ocean trenches are like Black holes. they are dark and unexplored.

Oceans and skies, both are vast and seem endless.

They are filled with mystery that we do not understand. Scientists discover new creatures in the oceans while new stars and planets are discovered in the space.

7. Star Story

Twinkle twinkle little star... it is my favourite nursery rhyme. It has always put me in infinite wonder.

According to NASA, a star is a self-luminous ball made up of very hot gases that is held together by its own gravity.

They come in different shapes and sizes

The closest star to our Earth is our own Sun.

The sun is the only source of light and heat that makes the flowers bloom. Life would not exist without it.

Like everything in nature, stars too are born, live out their lives and die. They have a life cycle.
Stellar Nebula
Red Giant
Primary Nebula
Average Star
White Dwarf
Massive Star
Neutron Star
Red Super Giant
Black Hole
Supernova

All stars originate from Stellar Nebula. These are massive clouds made up of hot gas and dust.

Nebulas are when a star begins its life. In the beginning it looks like different colors scattered around space also in an irregular shape. It is the beginning of a star's life.

It might become a massive star then a red super giant and then a supernova.
Or
An average star then a red giant.

A supernova is an enormous explosion that happens when a massive star reaches the end of it's life.

In the year 1054, a supernova happened very near the earth! It looked very big in the sky as a gigantic cloud.

Scientists around the world predict that one day our sun will be so big it will swallow every thing near it. **It will become a red gulping monster.**

In about 6 billion years from now, the Sun will become a red giant

Scientists at NASA predict that, one day our Sun will be so big, it will swallow Venus and Mercury! Whether it will swallow Earth, is still not clear.

This is because the Sun would age into gianthood

As the Sun would grow bigger, the temperatures would soar up and the Earth will not be a habitable planet. It might get toasted!

What do you think will happen if the temperature of the sun increases to unsafe levels?

All the water from the surface of the Earth and under it will get heated up and evaporated.

The glaciers will melt superfast.

There would be forest fires spreading and engulfing almost everything.

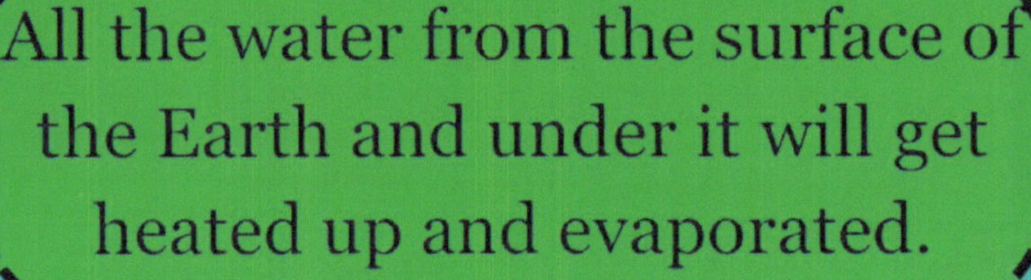

All the life forms will end.

9. Moon Tales

Scientists believe that the moon was formed when an object big enough, collided with earth, and pieces of Earth flew off into space. The biggest pieces clumped together and formed the moon.

The moon is 384,000 kilometers away from Earth.

Earth has just one moon. It is called Earth's natural satellite.

The Moon is one-fourth the size of Earth in width.

The Moon has a very thin and weak atmosphere, making it impossible for humans or any other living organism to survive independently. There is neither air to breathe nor sound to hear.

There are thousands of craters on the moon.

It takes 27.3 days for moon to orbit around earth.

According to NASA, the mean radius of the moon is 1737.5 kilometers

Craters are formed when meteoroids crash on its surface. They crash directly over its surface as there is no atmosphere to stop them.

The Moon has day and night, just like earth.

10. Moons of Jupiter

Planet Jupiter has some of the largest moons present in our solar system

Out of the 95 moons that Jupiter has, the largest are Ganymede, Callisto, IO and Europa.

They are called Galilean satellites after Italian astronomer Galileo Galilei, who is credited with their discovery in 1610.
He was the first to turn the telescope skywards.

Ganymede is the biggest moon in the solar system.

NASA's Hubble space telescope has discovered water on Ganymede's surface. There is an evidence of presence of an underground salt water ocean. It has more water than all the water on earth's surface.

Ganymede is bigger than Mercury.

Callisto is the second largest moon. It is the most heavily cratered object in our solar system.

IO is the third largest Jupiter's moon and is the most volcanically active world in our solar system.

Europa is Jupier's fourth largest moon. It is 90% the size of Earth's moon.

11. Gravity

Gravity holds the earth to the sun and moon to the earth. It keeps us from flying into the space as we jump or spin.

Sir Isaac Newton discovered the laws of gravity after observing apples fall from a tree.

Clocks closer to gravitational source will tick more slowly than the ones farther away. Reason, Earth's gravity is much weaker where the satellites orbit. This causes the clocks to run faster than the ones on Earth.

On the moon, gravity is about one sixth as strong as on earth. So astronauts can jump higher.

The Moon's gravity pulls on Earth's oceans, causing the tides to rise and fall.

Earth's gravity keeps us, the oceans, the atmosphere in place. Without it, everything would just drift into space.

Black holes have extremely strong gravity, so strong that not even light can escape its path.

This is because the matter has been pressed into a tiny space.

30

Why all the planets are round in shape?

All planets are round because of GRAVITY. A planet's gravity pulls it from all sides.

Gravity pulls from the center towards the edges. This makes the overall shape of the planet a sphere.

13. Black Holes

Scientists think that a black hole can be as small as an atom. however, they have a mass equal to a large mountain. Mass is the amount of matter in that object.

Black holes are invisible because no light can escape. Space telescopes with special tools can help find black holes.

There can be supermassive black holes too that can hold the mass of one million suns together.

Bigger black holes are called Stellar black holes that can have a mass more than 20 times the mass of the sun.

Our Milky Way too has a supermassive black hole in the center. it is called Sagittarius A. It has a mass equal to four million suns.

How does a black hole form?
Scientists think that the smallest black holes
formed when the universe began.

When a black hole
and a star come
closer, a high
energy light is
emitted which
cannot be seen by
human eyes.

Stellar black holes are
formed when the
center of a very big
star falls upon itself.

Scientists use telescopes
and satellites to observe
such black holes and stars.

When any object gets too close to
a black hole, it is squeezed
horizontally and stretched
vertically, resembling a noodle.

Can our Sun become a black hole? Will it eat Earth?

According to scientists, Sun cannot become a black hole as it is not a big enough star to become a black hole.

There is no black hole close enough to our solar system that can eat Earth.

If we replace the sun with an equal mass of a black hole, still the Earth will not fall into it because the black hole will have the same gravity as of sun. thus, earth will still revolve around it. The only problem would be the entire solar system would become cold as there would be no sun, no heat.

15. Comets

Comets are composed of dust, rocks and ices
They are cosmic snowballs that orbit the sun.

When comets get close to the Sun, they start to heat up, and that's when the magic happens. The heat causes the ice to vaporize, creating a glowing tail that can stretch millions of miles. This tail always points away from the Sun, making the comet look like it's blazing across the sky.

Comets like the Halley's comet will be visible in our sky in the year 2061 because it is visible in the sky of our earth every 72-80 years and it will be visible worldwide.

Some comets only visit the inner solar system every few hundred or even thousands of years, so spotting one is like witnessing a rare cosmic event. It's pretty epic to think about how something so ancient and far away can create such a beautiful sight in our sky.

The Kupier Belt and the Oort cloud are the two reservoirs of comets in the space.

As theorized by astronaut Gerard Kupier in 1951, Kupier Belt is a doughnut shaped region beyond the orbit of Neptune. It contains millions of icy bodies.

Some comets come from the Oort cloud which is spear shaped in the outer edge of the solar system.

Comets come out of the Kuiper Belt due to the gravitational interaction with other planets and collision between icy objects.

How are comets named?

According to International Astronomical Union Guidelines, comets are named after their discoverers or spacecraft or the telescope or observatory.

Most comets are named after astronomers who discovered them.

If more than one person discovers a comet independently, the comet may bear the name of multiple astronomers.

Halley's comet was discovered by Edmond Halley who claculated its orbit.

Comet Shoemaker- Levy 9 was discovered by Eugene Shoemaker, Carolyn Shoemaker and David Levy

17. Asteroids

Asteroids are like the leftover building blocks of the solar system that didn't quite make it into becoming a planet.

These are chunks of rock and metal just floating around in space.

Asteroids can be as small as a pebble or as big as a mountain.

Asteroids have all sorts of weird shapes—some look like potatoes, while others are more like lumpy boulders.

66 Million years ago, Chicxulub asteroid hit the Earth. According to scientists, the asteroid was 10 to 15 km in diameter.

The impact was so powerful that it created a crater, 150 km long in diameter.

The impact caused shock waves, tsunamis, ash, dust and steam clouds to blanket the Earth and blocked the sun rays.

As a result, the Earth plunged into cold and darkness. This duration is called impact winter. Scientists believe that 75% of species on Earth became extinct during this period. Dinosaurs were one of them.

18. Rogue Planets

I am starless!
I am alone. I do not have any star.
Dont worry guys! We are ROGUE PLANETS!
Are we expelled from our solar system?
NO! We ejected out! HA! HA! HA!
We are difficult to detect.
We float freely

19. Meteoroids

Sometimes asteroids smash into one another. As a result, small pieces of asteroid break off and are called METEOROIDS

When a meteoroid enters the Earth's atmosphere, it vaporizes and turns into a meteor.

It leaves a streak of light (glowing hot air) behind it as it zips through the atmosphere.

A meteor is also called a *space rock*.

When the earth encounters many meteoroids, it is called a Meteor Shower.

Meteoroids are small dust particles or the size of a boulder.

Don't worry! They quickly burn in the atmosphere. So there are very less chances that they would reach and hit the surface of the Earth.

The good news is, you do not need any telescope or go to a different location to watch them. you may watch the night sky from your garden or terrace and enjoy the delightful sight of the meteor shower.

20. Oceanic Planets

Space scientists are searching for planets which are composed mostly of water and a very little amount of land. Such planets are called Oceanic planets.

Scientists believe that many, many billion years ago, these planets had land. However, this cold land got submerged in hot boiling water.

21. THINK ZONE

Why are space scientists searching for water on other planets?

We all have studied in the school books that water is the fundamental element of life.

The very first life forms have originated in water.

Discovering water on other planets will give a new hope to find life beyond our Earth.

22. Time Travel! Is it Real?

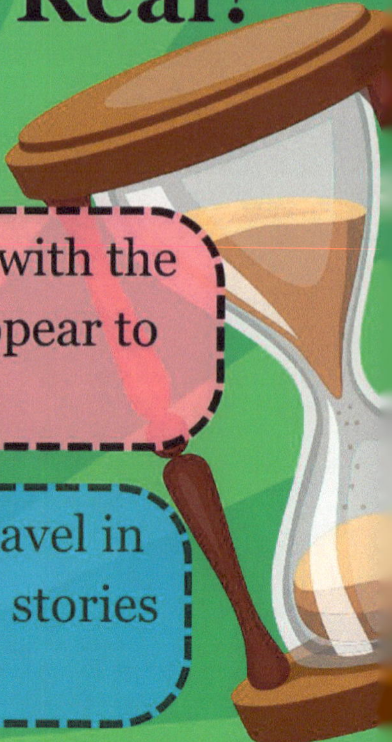

According to Einstein, if you travel with the speed of light; time on earth will appear to slow down.

You cannot use a time machine to travel in the future or past as shown in fiction stories and movies.

Speed of light is constant. Nothing can travel faster than light.

The speed of light is 299792458 m/s. So if you want to go in the future to see what you would be doing after 10 years from now, you should travel at this speed.

If you can travel with the speed of light, it would be possible for you to travel into the future.

Gravity affects time. If you read Albert Einstein's Theory of Relativity, you will realise that gravity curves space and time, which slows down the passage of time. This is called gravitational time dilation.

TIME TRAVEL is possible but not like the way shown in movies Here's the reality…

NASA's James Webb Space Telescope is regarded as the cosmic time machine.

It can capture ancient light that takes billions of years to reach Earth, allowing astronomers to look back in time..

Time traveling in the past

NASA's telescopes help scientists see stars and galaxies that are far away from us. It takes long time for the light from these galaxies to reach us. So next time when you look from the telescope you look what they looked like long time ago…actually you will look in the past of that star or galaxy.

23. Wormholes

A wormhole can be considered as a tunnel that cuts short the time required to travel and reach places.

You mean to say TELEPORTATION!

Wormholes can be considered like ultimate sci-fi shortcuts in space.

All you need to do is get equipped and zip off.

Amazing new universe here! Wowie!

We do not know whether wormholes really exist!

They are assumed to exist in theories of General Relativity that best explains the universe.

Imagine, if Earth goes from a big enough wormhole, it would send the Earth to another dimension. This new dimension would have new time, new laws of physics, new solar system and new galaxies!

24. Spacesuit Facts

Astronauts wear space suits. They are called Extravehicular Mobility Units

They are filled with air to create a pressure that is similar to Earth's atmosphere.

The spacesuits are heavy, almost 300 pounds approximately equal to 136.078 kilograms

They allow astronauts to move, work and survive in harsh space conditions.

In space, temperatures can swing from 250 degrees Fahrenheit to being super-cold at -250 degrees Fahrenheit.

Each space suit provides a backpack that supplies oxygen to breathe, removes carbon dioxide and stores water required to drink during spacewalks.

Astronaut gloves are thick for protection. However, they are flexible enough for astronauts to move their fingers and grip tools.

They are equipped with a gold coated visor to protect the astronaut's eyes from the intense rays of the sun.

The spacesuits have a built in communication system. They are equipped with a microphone and a speaker so that astronauts can communicate with each other.

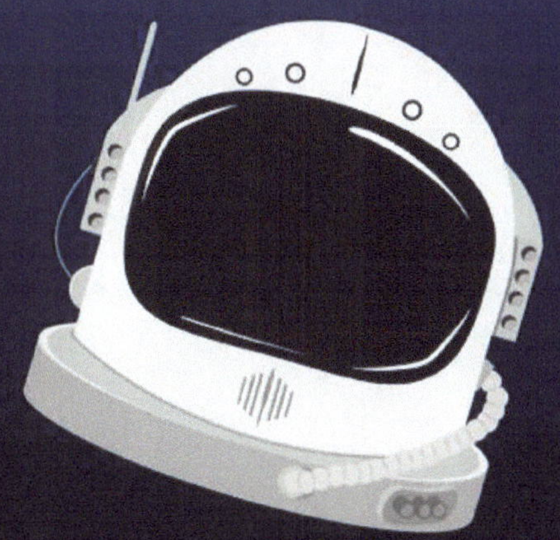

25. Spacecraft Facts

Spacecrafts are vehicles built for space travel. they are designed to work in the vacuum of space.

They are different from airplanes.

Some are like satellites, orbiting the Earth, others are like rovers that land on other planets.

Many spacecrafts do not have astronauts onboard. These are called unmanned spacecraft.

They cannot take off by themselves. They need powerful rockets to free them from Earth's gravity.

Rockets are called launch vehicles

Such spacecrafts are controlled from Earth.

Spacecrafts communicate with Earth using radio waves and a network of antennas and satellites.

The International Space Station is a giant spacecraft that orbits the Earth.

Spacecrafts are loaded with cameras, sensors and other devices to study planets, stars and other galaxies.

Astronauts live and work on it for months together.

They eat thermostabilized(heat processed to destroy micro organisms) and rehydratable(require water to be added before eating) foods. They also eat fresh fruits and vegetables.

25. THINK ZONE

Where do satellites in orbit get energy from?

They get energy from many sources like sun, batteries and nuclear resources

Satellites have solar panels that convert solar energy into electrical energy.

Spacecraft batteries also serve as one of the sources of power. These batteries are designed to work in tough environments. They need to be recharged several times.

Unstable atoms release energy as heat.

References

- Einstein. A , The Special and The General Theory, Time is an Illusion[2017] Fingerprint Publishing

- Hawking. S, Black Holes(L)- The Reith Lectures, [2016] Bantam Books

- Wonder House Books, Space Stars and Galaxies -Knowledge Encyclopedia for Kids[2020]

- www.spaceplace.nasa.gov

- www.science.nasa.gov

- Random books

- www. youtube.com- Random space videos